WHO YOU ARE

by Joseph Kloss

Not Two Press

Rochester, New York

Published by:

Not Two Press

P.O. Box 18572

Rochester, New York 14618

www.nottwopress.com

ISBN 978-0-9794568-1-7

LCCN 2007902209

This book is dedicated to you, to who you are.

CONTENTS

A Note to the Reader

A Note to the Reader

This book is written in second person in hopes that each of us will experience it in our true first person condition. This is the sort of state that might arise when someone says, "Hey, you!" and we reply, Who, me?" If we hear the confirmation, "Yes, you," we are apt to feel an intense self-consciousness; "That means me! I'm the one." In such a case, the second person address can lead to a distinctly first person state.

Second person also has the power to make us feel a sense of intimacy, as if someone very familiar is speaking directly to us, or as if, perhaps, we are speaking to ourselves, our separate selves. It is, in fact, in that part of us that feels separate from everything else, and there alone, that any confusion lies.

Beyond the separate self that we have come to believe in lies the immensity of our true identity; an absolute reality that cannot be otherwise.

INTRODUCTION

Most of us care about truth. We know inherently that truth is single and simple and the same for all conditions and for all time. Anything less is merely a relative truth and not admissible evidence in the court of reality, which accepts only the truth, the whole truth, and nothing but the truth. The search for absolute truth, a unified field theory of sorts, is the most worthwhile of adventures.

The good news:
There *is* a single and simple truth that, as you would expect of the truth, fits everything, everywhere, and every time.
The bad news:
Well, there is no bad news, except, perhaps, that what is finally real and true cannot be put into words.

The ineffable nature of truth projects the illusion of concealment, and yet common sense tells us that the truth must be everywhere, including right in front of us.
What to do?

The secret to finding something that has been lost or hidden is in knowing where to look. So here are a few whispered words telling you exactly where to look.

PART I

WHO YOU ARE

You are the one.

This book has been created specifically for you.

You are not the only person who will read this book, but you are the one for whom it is intended.

This book is a living thing. It is composed of billions of organized particles, a veritable universe unto itself, and it contains within it the distilled insights of literally thousands of years of wisdom teachings. It exists for a single purpose: to offer you the opportunity to awaken from the dream that you think of as your life, and to point out the reality of reality, the utter verity that is the heart of your being.

Who You Are

Word to thought to insight to knowing to being; this is the course of the river of these words. These words will not speak in the same way to anyone else who may read or hear them. These words are meant for you.

This book has come into being to help you realize the truth about who you are:

Imagine that you are someone who is searching. In this case, imagine that you are searching for your misplaced eyeglasses.

Truth is the eyeglasses that make it possible for you to see while you are looking for the eyeglasses that you *think* you have lost, forgetting that if they were not already in use, you could not see to search for them. This is the truth of who you are.

The words that follow are meant to show how this is so.

ARE YOU?

The subject of this book is who you are. But first, before examining who you are, maybe you should ask yourself *if* you are.

One of the most fundamental questions a human being can ask is one that is seldom considered. Some things seem so obvious that there is no need even to wonder about them. But the question remains: Are you?

Think about it.

Feel it out.

Are you?

Who You Are

Okay, it's a silly question. Of course you are, or at least *something* is. You might not be very clear ab out what is happening, but whatever it is, it is not nothing.

Yet, have you ever stopped to ponder this silly question and especially to consider the implications of an affirmative answer?

You have probably thought about other big questions:
Who am I?
Why am I here?
What's it all about?

But the question of whether you exist doesn't arise because you *know* you are; you can feel your own presence, your existence.

Are You?

The question of your existence does not arise because there is something about you that is immediate and actual, something unmistakable.

Your thoughts and feelings may be all over the map and your sense of identity may be in perpetual flux, but *something* is happening and, whatever it is and whatever it means, it cannot be denied that it is happening to you, in you, and as you.

For want of a better word, you can call it your being.

After all, you are a human being, and since you are a being, it follows that you *are* being.

You are.

WHO ARE YOU?

You are.

Who you are is another matter entirely and one that has intrigued humankind for millennia. It is the most essential of questions, and perhaps the most frustrating, because ultimately there is no answer to this question that is communicable in words. Yet a specific injunction persists throughout human history, always the same advice:

"Know Thyself."

The wisdom traditions of every age are joined here in one accord: find out who you are, look inside. If you want to know the most important thing there is to know, look nowhere else but within yourself.

Who You Are

The ancients implore you to undertake this adventure, to look deep inside, to know yourself.

What self? Which self? Instead of asking "Who am I?" perhaps the question should be "*What* am I?" There seem to be so many parts, so many facets, so many selves. How should you look? What should you look for?

You are a thinking person, a feeling person, an intuitive person. You have goals and dreams, needs and desires, abilities and shortcomings. You are both rational and instinctive, confident, and cautious. You know the feeling of pleasure and you may know something of joy and peace, but you are also no stranger to pain and fear; and sometimes, deep inside, you feel what is in your heart.

So, in the midst of all these components and qualities, who are you?

WHO YOU ARE NOT

Whatever ideas you may have about your identity are necessarily mistaken. They are mistaken because they are partial. The truth of who you are cannot be put into words, cannot be contained in concepts or feelings or even intuitions.

You are not what you appear to be. You are not a biological organism that has become conscious of itself. You are not made up of elements.

And here's the problem: your mind is an inadequate tool for exploring the truth of who you are and is, in fact, the source of your mistaken identity. Your mind has assembled your perceptions and thoughts into concepts that have become your knowledge of yourself, and this accumulated knowledge has been summarily promoted to the rank of reality.

Who You Are

Your image of reality, no matter how informed and sophisticated, is just a symbol, a representation born of imagination. How could it be otherwise?

There can be nothing that appears in your mind that is not a concept, a mental image, a construct. It is therefore unrealistic to expect that you can apprehend the whole truth about anything at all through the agency of your mental processes.

To imagine that your powers of perception are sufficient to reveal the actuality of any single thing in all its dimensions and qualities is evidence of a gross misunderstanding of the nature of...nature.

Who You Are Not

A survey of the history of science reveals occasions when specific fields of research had been thought to be "completed," only to discover in succeeding months or years or centuries that science had barely scratched the surface of what there is to know about even the most humble areas of study.

This being the case, how likely is it that whatever you know about yourself thus far is also incomplete?

Science is simply one the most concrete examples of the age-old truism that the more you know, the more you realize how little you know.

Who You Are

It is only natural that you have been led to a mistaken sense of your identity. Every experience of your life has made it obvious that who you are or, rather, who you think you are, began at a very specific time and place. You have been alive for thousands of days leading right up to this moment and you have paperwork to prove it.

You have a continuity of experience which is undeniable. You can call as witnesses many people who will testify that you have done this and that and been here and there, that you *are* somebody.

You have spent a lifetime accumulating and interpreting your experiences and relationships, defining yourself, developing an identity, cultivating a persona, a look, a personal philosophy, a set of values, and a code of conduct, creating a style all your own. In short, you have assumed your rightful place in the universe. Very naturally then, this is who you take yourself to be.

Who You Are Not

But the assumptions you have made about yourself are based on faulty data and are thus incomplete and misleading. They make sense to you because you usually have no reason to call them into question.

Your "knowledge" of yourself keeps you from knowing who you are.

Drawing from your life experiences, your mind has assembled and organized a body of circumstantial evidence, constructed a conceptual framework, and welded the boundaries of reality into place; boundaries beyond which you generally have no need to venture.

Any time you have had occasion to expand the limits of your understanding, you have assembled a new assortment of concepts that are consistent with your more recent ideas. But your new image of reality will always be less than the whole truth, for nothing the mind can conceive can approach the actuality of what is finally so.

Who You Are

In the meantime, here you are, reading this book, breathing in and out, and feeling very much the way you normally feel. How is it possible that your image of yourself could be so far off the mark?

You have a lifetime's accumulation of seemingly incontrovertible facts that make it evident that you are somebody. For starters, you can see that you have a body. You can think, so you obviously have a mind. You have a name and there is a picture on your identification card or drivers license that at least remotely resembles who you take yourself to be.

You have had many memorable experiences throughout your life, varying from okay to really, really good, and from not-so-good to nightmarish, and maybe even worse. You survived your childhood and adolescence, though not unscathed, and now you are who you have become.

Who You Are Not

The whole of your lifetime of experiences and choices has made you, for better or worse, who you are. Now people recognize you, more or less, for who you are and you are seldom mistaken for anyone else.

WHO YOU SEEM TO BE

Since you appear to be some-body, take a few moments to examine the body that you seem to be.

It is obvious that there is a body. Except for sleep and the occasional reverie, it is with you all the time. It *is* you all the time. It is your arms and legs, your height and weight, your face in the mirror. Not only can you touch it, you touch *with* it, you see and hear with it, you live in the world within it, and you would not be where you are without it.

There may be room for argument about when life begins, but there is little disagreement about the reality of the physical body. It is concrete and indisputable evidence of your existence as a human being.

Who You Are

So where are you in this body?

Science tells you that your head is command central. Your brain is where your thinking happens and where the majority of your senses are located. So why, when you refer to yourself by pointing, do you point to your chest, to your heart? Could that be where you truly reside? Surely it is someplace central. It's not as if you exist primarily in your hands or your feet. And if you *are* located in the brain, then where in the brain? Are you contained in some primal location in the brain stem, or are you the product of the higher order functions of the neocortex? And if so, then where in the neocortex? Prefrontal perhaps? Or maybe you think of yourself as existing everywhere in the brain at once. You might even think of yourself as existing everywhere in the body at once. Well, how does that work? Where do you begin and where are your edges? Do you stop at the surface of the skin or do you consider the energy fields generated by the body to be part of you as well?

Who You Seem to Be

How does your mind fit in? After all, it is with the mind that you decide *whatever* you decide about who you are. Your mind is the witness, mediator, judge and jury, and literally creates your world by interpreting the data that it selects from among the myriad data to which it is exposed.

Since you spend all of your waking time and much of your sleeping time listening to your mind's ongoing monologue, it may seem more likely that your true identity is to be found in your mind rather than in your body.

Your mind does your thinking for you. It attempts to incorporate the mental images and the physical sensations that abound in your internal and external environment, and tries to keep the peace when emotions threaten to overrun the mental machinery.

Who You Are

What about emotions? Are they closer to the truth of who you are? Are they mental or are they more physical, or some of each, and in what proportions?

Sometimes your feelings can tell you more about who you are than your mind or your body. Are they more trustworthy? Are they more you?

There is also the time problem. You already know that this body is not going to survive for much more than one hundred years and, even if you are relatively young, you have seen enough to know that your body could become a corpse before you have another opportunity to take off your shoes.

Who You Seem to Be

What about death? What happens when the body malfunctions or wears out, as it surely will?

All of the unique qualities that make you who you are will exist only in the memory of your survivors and in assorted pieces of physical evidence that probably won't last very long either.

So what about you? What will happen to you?

The body dies. The machine stops running, but it doesn't go anywhere. All of the materials that are present when the body is alive are still there when the body is without life. The only thing that is missing is life, the animating principle, and you.

What about you?

Who You Are

If you imagine your physical body to be the entirety of who you are, then upon the death of the body, you probably expect to disappear, snuffed out like the flame of a candle.

If you think that your mind is distinct from the body, then you may have an image of your mind somehow continuing after the body dies. You may believe in an afterlife, equating your mental and emotional life with the concept of a soul. You may imagine the continuation of your existence taking place in some metaphysical dimension. Depending on your cultural conditioning, you may have a fairly specific set of expectations for what will happen to whatever you are after you have left the body.

But can you see how these are all ideas? All of your concepts, beliefs, hopes, and expectations are created by the mind. And so, by the way, is everything else.

MIND

From well before you were born you have been receiving, interpreting, and responding to sensory impressions. Initially, your innate biological faculties handled your interactions with your environment, but it was not long before your unique personal qualities began to influence your relationship to this new world. Soon you were a complete physical, mental, emotional, and social human being; an individual.

From the very beginning until this moment, you have lived your life in your mind. As your eyes focus upon the printed symbols on this page or your ears attend to these sounds you think of as words, and while your mental faculties review your vast history of personal experience to assign meanings to these symbols, right now, in the midst of all this sensory and mental activity, you can feel your mind in action.

Who You Are

There is much more going on in your mind than gathering and interpreting information. This awareness that is present in exactly this moment, as you are processing these words, is the very same awareness that has been present during every single physical, mental, and emotional experience of your life – first word, first step, first crossroad, first rude awakening, first big question, first epiphany.

The awareness that is attending to these words is constantly present, but seldom appreciated.

Awareness is usually obscured by the objects it illuminates.

Sensations, thoughts, and feelings captivate the attention so readily, and entertain so thoroughly, that there is room for little else.

Anyway, you have other responsibilities; your job has always been to stay in control of your life and to make the best possible judgments and choices for yourself and for those people and things you care about.

Mind

It is natural that you feel that you are in control of how you make decisions and respond to situations, but the vast majority of your sensory and mental activity takes place without your conscious participation.

The visual image of this page that your eyes are seeing is the product of innumerable neural processes that do not end in the occipital lobe but require processing and interpretation from other areas of the brain as well. With every sound you hear, your brain is calling upon the memories of similar sounds you have heard for purposes of identification and evaluation, i.e., is this a sound that requires attention?

Who You Are

The vast majority of your physical and mental processes, and your emotional life, happen beneath the level of your waking consciousness. Those mental phenomena that reach the surface of your awareness have gone through a host of complex screening processes. Once these impressions have come to your attention you can watch them go through other evaluations as you "think about" the things that arise in consciousness.

Thinking creates your reality and binds you to it. Thoughts come and go of their own accord and define your world for you because you believe that the thoughts that appear in your mind are *your* thoughts.

Thinking is the lock. Awareness is the key.

The awareness that is present in this and every moment is *the timeless witness* of all the sensations that arise in you, all the experiences that happen in you and to you.

•

Mind

Every experience you have ever had, no matter how commonly shared with other people, has been your own experience.

More than once in your life you have probably had a clear sense that no one knows the real you. Indeed, even if you were born with a womb-mate, you were born by yourself and, eventually, you will die by yourself.

Every sensation you have ever had – physical, mental, or emotional, has been yours alone. No human being, no matter how close to you, can ever truly know your innermost thoughts and feelings.

No matter how heroically you attempt to communicate your inner experience, you cannot adequately articulate how you feel or who you are.

Words cannot describe you.

Who You Are

Nothing can convey who you are to anyone else, nor can your most comprehensive thoughts contain who you are, even for the sake of your *own* understanding. You can feel it and you can try to think about it, but it will never be possible for your mind to comprehend who you are.

Thoughts cannot contain you.

When you look within, it is often difficult to make a clear distinction between thoughts and feelings, as each is constantly generating the other. Your emotions and your thoughts, and the many sensory impressions that find their way into your field of awareness, are all eventually assimilated by the mind. The mind is the mediator, the arbiter of your relationship to the world.

Mind

The world you live in is your own world. It takes its reality from your experiences and from your inner relationship *to* those experiences. How you think and feel about things makes all the difference, no matter what the differences are.

Your body and this world in which your body exists are perceived and interpreted entirely by the mind. Your mind has assigned very specific definitions and meanings to the things that exist in your world.

While it may appear that you hold many of these perceptions and ideas in common with other people, the only thing you can know directly is the content of your own consciousness.

As far as your personal experience is concerned, there *is* no other consciousness.

Who You Are

All you have ever known, all you can ever know, is your own experience.

You can never experience anything that is outside of your own consciousness.

Your body may be sitting in a classroom or caught in a cloudburst, but your experience takes place in consciousness.

Everything is in consciousness. When you get right down to it, that could be what you are: consciousness. You can feel it right now. You can feel the sensation of being the witness of the things that are going on in your environment and in your body, and especially in your mind.

Mind

Whatever else you may say about who you are, you are a presence, you are here, and there is a sense in which you are the same right now as you have always been.

Your body has certainly changed from infancy to childhood to wherever you seem to be today. You probably think and feel differently about many things than you used to, but there is something fundamental about you that has not changed.

There is something real and abiding about you that is entirely beyond words.

It is not surprising that you find it difficult to describe this unchanging part of you. It is the real you, and completely beyond anyone's ability to comprehend with the mind. But you can *feel* it, and as you know, your feelings are often more accurate and more trustworthy than your thoughts.

YOU

So what is it about you that has not changed? What is this underlying presence that seems so familiar, that seems so "you?"

It cannot be your body. Your body has changed radically over the years and bears little resemblance to the tiny character that got "you" started.

It has just been suggested that it is your consciousness that is the source of your experience. Can it be that simple? Could it be even simpler?

The way to find out is to perform a little experiment: look and see.

Look very carefully and keep looking until you see.

Who You Are

You can begin this experiment from precisely where you are. Bring your attention to bear on your sense perceptions, beginning with whatever is most noticeable and progressively attending to each of your senses in turn until you feel fully aware of yourself right where you are. Vision and hearing may be the easiest, but watch for the subtleties of contrasts and colors and listen for faint and distant sounds. Feel how gravity pulls your body, feel the touch of the clothes on your skin. Are you able to taste anything? Can you detect any odors?

Now take your attention off your body, which is just another part of the outside world, and turn your attention back upon itself.

Turning your attention inward may put you in unfamiliar territory. It is like entering a dark room. At first you can't see anything at all, but as your perception adjusts to the change, things begin to come into focus. If you stay with it for long enough you may be able to see fairly well.

So what do you see when you look within?

You

As you begin to see beyond the initial darkness, you will become aware of thoughts and sense perceptions arising and receding, usually being replaced immediately by other mental objects. At the same time, underlying the parade of objects, is the consciousness in which they appear.

This consciousness is often likened to the ocean upon the surface of which the waves of the mind rise and fall. Take a few moments to observe how this works in your mind. Watch the mental objects appear on the surface of consciousness and disappear as other waves arise.

Occasionally, you may notice periods in which the waves subside and you can get a better look at the consciousness in which they arise.

Gradually you can begin to discriminate between these two parts of yourself: the waves of thought and other mental objects, and the oceanic ground in which they have their existence.

Who You Are

Consider the implications of the suggestion that the thoughts and feelings that you have always taken to be your defining characteristics are just the beginning, just a tiny point in an infinite expanse, just the very surface of an unfathomable depth.

In these depths, things are very different from what takes place on the surface, and yet this depth is just as much a part of you as your innermost thoughts and feelings which, in reality, rise from the infinity that you are.

Exploring the heights and depths of consciousness can reveal knowledge and understanding beyond all imagining.

But even consciousness is not sufficient to encompass your true identity.

You

Recall the beginning of this "look and see" exercise. You began by looking within and gradually coming around to the observation of thoughts and sensations, not as things in themselves but just as mental objects. Eventually you were able to distinguish between the waves of mental objects rising and falling and the ocean of consciousness in which they subsist.

Now, in this moment, as you rest here in the presence of the thoughts that are arising in consciousness, you are in a position to appreciate consciousness itself, which in this and every moment underlies and supports all mental activity.

You are the witness of the objects that arise in consciousness.

You are the witness of the consciousness in which all objects arise.

Who You Are

For your whole life you may have imagined that the things you think and feel define who you are. You have assumed your identity as a result of the unique thoughts and feelings that you have experienced, thoughts and feelings that can be experienced by no one else.

In this very moment, thoughts are appearing in consciousness. You are the witness of these thoughts

They may be your thoughts, but they are not you.

You are the being in which consciousness appears. This consciousness that you are experiencing in this moment does not exist in your mind; your mind exists in this consciousness, and this oceanic consciousness exists because of the being that you are.

When you look at yourself in this way you may not be able to see much, but you can probably feel something. You can feel yourself. You can feel your own presence, your existence. You can feel this *being* that makes you a human being.

You

Continue to point your powers of observation in your own direction. You naturally experience thoughts and other mental objects arising and receding, being replaced by other objects. You can also appreciate the presence of the witness of those objects. Objects appear and witnessing happens.

You are happening. You are the witness. Who else could it be? Only you could be watching your own thoughts.

Do you notice what happens when you focus attention on the witness, when you try to watch the watcher? All you can see are the objects that arise.

What you have always thought of as your mind is just a succession of mental objects and *you* are nowhere to be found.

You cannot see the witness.
You cannot see yourself.

Who You Are

When you look into you own mind, you discover that the mind is invisible. Except for the images that arise within it, there is nothing there.

What you have always thought of as your mind, your inner self, is really nothing but infinite space, a cloudless sky, a boundless capacity that becomes visible only when an object appears within it. If no object appears in your consciousness, there is nothing to be seen.

No thoughts, no mind.

When looking into your own consciousness, thoughts are found to be transient and insubstantial. Often, the most tangible thing you will find is in the domain of feelings. You can feel the actuality of this presence that you are. Even though you cannot apprehend it in the way you usually perceive objects, you can feel a reality to your presence, your being, that is not shared by other perceptions.

You

You have always thought that you were a human being because you have a human body. You have always thought you were a conscious being because you have a human brain.

Take another look inward. Feel the quality of the witnessing that happens when you look for yourself.

First of all, there is really nothing you can point to and say that you see yourself. There are thoughts, but they are not who is looking. You can't see who is looking because the eye cannot see itself. You cannot see yourself because you are who is looking.

You cannot see yourself in a mirror because mirrors show you only images, appearances that are "out there."

You will never see yourself by looking in a mirror because what you can see is not who you are.

Who You Are

You are not what you see when you look in a mirror.
You are that which sees what you see when you look in a
mirror.

PART II

WHO YOU ARE

In the course of examining who you are not, you have been exposed to several statements that point to who you are.

First of all, you *are*. You are a presence that can neither be denied nor escaped. In fact, you are not just *a* presence, one among many, you are presence itself.

You think that you are a human being, but in reality you are being itself, which just happens for the moment to appear to be human. The human part of you may be relatively short-lived, but your true being is another story altogether.

Who You Are

Becoming aware of who you are requires a revolution in perception, a radical reevaluation of how you look at yourself and, more importantly, what you see.

Who you are is nothing "out there" that can be viewed objectively. Even your subjective impressions of yourself are rendered objective in the moment they are noticed because *you* see them.

All the things you think and feel yourself to be cannot be who you are because they are all seen *by* you. So if all that you see and think and feel about yourself is not you, who are you?

You are the witness. You are the seer of everything seen. In reality, you are not even the seer; you are the seeing. You are not a person who is aware, *you are awareness*. You are the single and unchanging presence in which everything happens. You are the truth of existence. You are life itself.

You are what is.

Who You Are

Right now, in this moment, you can feel the ringing of truth in these words. You can feel the being that you are, directly, before thoughts arise. Stop for a moment and feel this being that brings everything into existence

Perhaps you are saying to yourself, "I can't feel it." If you think you can't feel it, check your pulse; do you feel your pulse? That's it! The *awareness* of your pulse, *this* awareness that you are right now, is it. This is being.

This being is who you are. This utter simplicity is who you are. This indescribable presence is who you are.

Realization means recognizing that this immediate and inescapable presence, this timeless and infinite being, exists not only within you, but *as* you.

Self-realization consists in honestly and humbly and finally admitting to yourself that you are not *a* being, one among many, you *are* being.

Who You Are

All your life you have been looking out at your world and your universe from the vantage point of your own consciousness, but now as you gaze in your own direction it is as if you have stepped back from the world and turned around to find yourself standing at the edge of a precipice.

At first it may seem like this being that you are discovering is a huge abyss, a dimensionless void, and to let yourself go into this emptiness would be to step off into oblivion. But that is only the way it appears.

When everything is seen at once, it looks, at first, like nothing.

Who You Are

The fullness that is reality takes the shape of emptiness, which contains everything. Each arises from the other. Each is the other.

So when you look into your own being your initial experience is one of emptiness, which turns out to be utter totality.

To get a better idea of how this works, summon up what you know about the vastness of the physical universe. Take a moment right now.

Try to imagine the whole of the universe all at once.

Who You Are

See what happens when you try to imagine infinity? Individual concepts, no matter how inclusive, cannot contain it. The attempt to conceive of everything at once takes the mind to its limits. Eventually, as the focus grows wider and deeper, the mind falls silent.

You may notice that while training your attention outward onto something as inconceivable as the universe, you find yourself gazing into that selfsame void that appeared earlier when you turned your attention around to look in your own direction.

It turns out that there is nothing you can point to and say, "This is who I am." Unless, of course, you spread your arms wide, open your mind to the infinite and incomprehensible All, and say, "This is who I am."

WHAT YOU ARE

Years ago, science began to point in this same direction by looking deeply into matter and discovering that there is nothing material, just a conglomeration of unimaginably tiny quanta of energy which, for want of a better word, were called particles. These particles exhibit what science refers to as a tendency to exist and they are separated by relative distances so vast that they render even dense matter essentially nothing but empty space.

Even the gross level of material existence that you think of as the world is constructed almost entirely of emptiness.

In the same way, who you really are is the whirling dance of emptiness and form, of everything and nothing, of being and not being.

Who You Are

Turn your attention again to the feeling of being, to the simple sensation of existence, right here, in this moment.

As you relax into your own presence you can feel your mind come and go. You may feel a subtle pulsation of your physical and mental energies as you relax into the ground from which everything arises. In one moment you are feeling the expansiveness of being and in the next moment you are thinking about what you are feeling.

If you are willing and able to release these thoughts and refocus your attention, you can return again to the subtle sense of being that is the core of who you are. Now, in this very moment, everything is as it is.

In the next moment your mind reappears, becoming conscious of the timeless condition that was your state in the preceding moment and "you" begin again.

What You Are

During the moment of pure being, "you," the person you have always thought yourself to be, disappears.

You go from form to emptiness, from consciousness to what could pass for unconsciousness.

You go from being "yourself" to a kind of not-being.

In such a moment, it is as if you are nothing, and yet, in that same moment, you are everything…all at once.

You may have heard descriptions of this emptiness and imagined it to be a philosophy of extinction, a kind of death, an ending of one's self. If your exposure to this notion examines only the nothingness, it is easy to see how this interpretation might arise. But perhaps by now you have come to appreciate how this image misses the point, how it misses the fullness, the everything-ness that can be experienced in no other way.

Who You Are

Take another moment to recall the sense of your ever-present being. Choose in this moment to withdraw your attention from your current mental activity and focus again upon the witness, upon your own spaciousness, the pure being that is the essence of what you are.

Allow yourself to experience the feeling that attends this awareness of your own infinity.

Now, do you experience a sensation of dread or looming annihilation?

More likely you feel an actuality, a directness of experience that, while it cannot be accurately described, feels familiar and comfortable. If you make the choice to spend some time exploring this feeling of presence, you may discover that it feels like home.

What You Are

In this moment of simple being you are free of the usual identifications that determine who you are and how it all is, and yet you are clearly and deeply present. But you are present without the baggage, without all the extras that made you who you thought you were.

In a moment like this you just are. In a moment like this you are not a female or a male, you are not even a human being. You are what you really are.

You are being.

So in a way, the direct knowledge of your true being *does* lead to a sort of death, a dissolution of who you have always taken yourself to be; but it may be more evident by now that you are not losing yourself, you are finding your Self.

SELF KNOWLEDGE

When you experience the infinite fullness/emptiness that lies just behind your physical and mental life, you are glimpsing your real identity. The meaning of truth is rooted in what you are.

You are real, the only certainty.

The being that you are is being itself.

The occasional return to the awareness of your own simple being, the being that you are in this and every moment, is all that is necessary to transform every aspect of your life.

Just this easily you find yourself experiencing small glimmers of a joyful homecoming and you realize that you are both the one who is coming home and the one to whom you are returning.

Who You Are

As you begin to abide for short periods in the reality of your own timeless presence, the misconceptions of a lifetime begin to fall away.

You are likely to find yourself spontaneously behaving in ways that are more consistent with who you really are; not who you thought you would be or wish you could be, but the simple truth of who you always already are.

You may well ask how this happens. How is it that you begin to feel more authentic, more spontaneous, more real?

It is the natural result of finally allowing yourself to *be,* without pretense or preference, free from every effort or desire to be anything or anyone in particular.

Self Knowledge

You can become more familiar with the sensation of immediate being by creating an environment that supports it. Take some time each day to look beyond all your notions of your life in the world, your life in your home, your life in the body. Bring the mind to rest and return to this spacious stillness, this resounding silence in which the clear light of being reveals the truth that cannot be spoken or even thought, but which can be known directly as you dissolve into that which is.

The practice of self-knowledge does not require a daily renewal of the search for your true self. Once you have recognized that you are the changeless witness of everything that arises within and without, you lose the urge to look for yourself, because you understand that you cannot see the seer.

You will never see what you are; you can only *be* what you are.

Who You Are

Any time you attempt to see yourself you may be sure that whatever you see is not who you are.

There are not two of you, one looking upon the other. There is no one to see who you are because you are the seeing. You are not an individual who is aware of yourself. You are awareness.

Imagine how many times you have heard it said: "All is one." This is the meaning of non-duality. This is the reality of existence, the truth of life.

It is only in the being/awareness that you are in this moment that the universe arises. From a personal point of view it may seem presumptuous and arrogant, but consider it from your own experience: no you, no universe. The universe has its being in the awareness that you are.

All is one.

You *are* that one.

Self Knowledge

Feel the oneness that is the foundation of this moment. Feel your intimate connection to everything that is. Feel the fullness and freedom that contains every single thing and appears as nothing at all.

When your mind is still you understand that you are not the person whose name you bear. You are that formless, objectless awareness of being/nonbeing from which all existences are projected and into which they all dissolve. You are that nameless identity that you have felt forever.

Your own true self *is* this infinite being that is beyond all knowing, beyond the subtlest feeling, beyond everything, *before* everything.

So you see, you can never know your true self. Who you are is entirely beyond that which can be known.

This is the essence of self-knowledge.

Once you realize that you cannot understand, you begin to understand.

Who You Are

You are the same as you have always been, the timeless awareness that you have always known in your heart.

You *are* the heart and this heart is nothing other than reality in the world of form.

The heart is being; being in and as the world.

It is called love.

It is what you are.

SCIENCE

This book is about you.

How would you classify such a book? Is this a philosophy or psychology book, a spiritual book? Could it be a religious book?

If you happened upon this book in a book store, you may have found it in the section on spirituality. If you understand spirit to mean the living principle that animates you and supports your conscious existence, then you could think of this as a spiritual book.

You could also think of this as a philosophy book. There are a great many philosophers and philosophies in the world that analyze and theorize about every imaginable topic from the obscure to the mundane; but if you take the word "philosophy" to its roots, then this is clearly a book of philosophy. The Greek *philos* (love) and *sophia* (wisdom) define the aspirations of this book.

Who You Are

Psychology? Well, returning again to word origins, *psyche* translates as soul or spirit. If psychology is indeed the study of the psyche, then this could be considered a resource text for study in the relatively new field of transpersonal psychology.

A religious book? If by religion you refer to cultivating a devotional relationship to the spiritual reality that constitutes your existence, then this could be thought of as a religious book.

If by religion you are thinking of an organized system of doctrines and beliefs relating to this spirit, then this is not an especially religious book. There is no call or need for beliefs here. This book simply points to what always is and invites you to look. It is neither necessary nor recommended that you should believe anything you read here except as you find it to be so in your own experience. Even then, belief is a tricky proposition. An open mind and an open heart will serve you better.

Science

There is another way to think of this book. Although seriously stretching the boundaries of plausibility, you might consider this to be a science book.

Going back again to the Latin root will help: *scire, sciens,* (to discern, to distinguish, to know.) That is what this book is about, discernment. It also offers a hypothesis of sorts and invites you to prove or disprove it by experimentation.

The proposition is that your initial knowledge of your truest identity has been skewed by the limited data available to you. In this book you are being introduced or reintroduced to supplementary information that provides you with another perspective and encourages a new appreciation of existing data.

You are also being invited to perform an experiment to determine whether there is validity to the contention that your true identity is off the charts.

Who You Are

If this book were to persist with this dubious claim to be a science book, it could cite a large number of experimenters, past and present, who would support this hypothesis.

As you might expect, most of these "experimenters" come not from scientific or academic communities but from religious and spiritual traditions. These saints and sages, yogis, monks, nuns and laypersons claim authority in this area of study because they undertook the necessary preparations, performed the requisite experiments, and arrived at similar conclusions.

What does all this mean? Simply that the information that is in this book, however far-fetched it may appear to be, cannot be ignored just because it is unusual.

It is patently unscientific to disallow a proposition simply because it seems too good to be true.

GOD

From the very first sentence, this book is about you. It begins by examining what you are not and invites you to consider what remains after you have been relieved of your conventional identity. If what remains turns out to be formless and nameless, what's the point?

There are many people who feel that the question of your identity is unimportant. From this point of view you are insignificant in the greater scheme of things and the only important thing in life is God, by whatever name God is called. God is everything and your true purpose in life is God's purpose. Your reason for being is to live a life that will be in harmony with God. Your goal in life is to grow to know God and perhaps even to aspire to become as God-like as the human condition will allow.

Who You Are

If you believe that God is all you **need** to know, do not imagine that you will find God in any holy **place** or in any holy book or collection of teachings or **prescription** of rituals or even in good works.

If you think you are worthy to approach God only through the intervention of another being, someone like Jesus the Christ, Mohammed the Prophet, Gautama the Buddha, or some other spiritual intermediary, you will eventually discover that, however earnest and devoted you may be, you have misinterpreted the true teaching and created distance where there is none. Taking your cues from the people around you, you have *set God apart* and then busied yourself in an earnest search to find that which seems to be missing in your life.

All the while, in one way or another, God's incarnation or God's emissary continuously repeats to you, "The Kingdom of Heaven is within," and you reply, "Yes, but where?"

God

To know God, to be enlightened, to experience that state of consciousness known variously as self-realization, awakening, illumination, transcendence, liberation... to see the light; all these and many other terms refer to the apprehension of levels of being which are entirely incommunicable and infinitely beyond even the most poetic of expressions.

Some thousands among the billions of human beings who have lived on this planet have attained not just glimpses of reality but a stable transcendence to a more highly developed level of being. Those who are known to us are uniform in their assertion that absolute reality is beyond comprehension or expression. They are also in agreement that the truth that is revealed in a vision of reality carries with it the truth of your real identity and your place in the scheme of things.

Reality, beyond all description and comprehension, brings final confirmation to the ancient declaration that all is one.

Who You Are

If all is one and you, as this book insists, are that one, where does God fit in?

This is especially relevant since all major religions that employ the concept of a god or gods acknowledge eventually that there is only one of it and that it includes everything. The spiritual traditions and the mystical branches of the major religions are unequivocal in their proclamation of the oneness of everything, and most of the world's religions ascribe their word for God to this oneness.

At the same time, human beings have assigned so many meanings to the concept of God that the word has nearly lost its meaning. Disfigured by myth, dogma and presumption, the word "God" has been exiled to a semantic wilderness.

Now, as always, God has as many meanings as there are minds to conceive the term, and all the while the true meaning of the word "God" remains beyond any conception and most certainly beyond any definition.

God

The fathers of the Jewish faith were attempting to communicate the unthinkable nature of God by employing a name which is unpronounceable, unspeakable. Indeed, the truth cannot be spoken.

The word "God" has been colored and discolored by so many meanings that it may be simpler to think of God with the help of another term altogether, a term that also, like God, refers to the truth of life.

God, by whatever name, is how things are.

God is what is.

God is reality.

NOT TWO

In order to consider the subject of God as reality it will be helpful to consider the issue of the two and the one, sometimes referred to in philosophical terms as dualism and nondualism. While the terms may seem self-explanatory, there is an important point here that can tell you more about who you are.

When the concept of God arises, duality arises with it. Duality means two; you here and God there, or, more commonly, you down here and God...up there.

The very existence of God presupposes the two of you, and yet the mystical traditions insist that it is possible for you to become one with God.

Nonduality means *not* two.

Who You Are

Over the course of your life you have been exposed to many explanations about God. You have heard that God is within you and you have heard that God is one. You have also read here, if nowhere else, that *you* are one, and not just one among many, but one without a second.

When you relax into the vastness of your true being, all individualities are absorbed into this being, your sense of separateness dissolves and you are all of a piece.

You are the presence in which everything appears and disappears.

So when the matter of God is introduced, nondualism might describe it this way: There is only God. There is nothing but God. There is no second thing in existence. All that appears to be emanates from, exists in, and dissolves back into the oneness that is God.

Not Two

Just a few pages earlier you were reading these same things about yourself. Does that mean you are God?

No, you are not God. Any time you experience yourself as a separate individual, you experience yourself as other than God. Considered as two, God is God and you are you. Seen as one, God *is* that one which is All and you have disappeared into that one like a raindrop in the ocean.

You are not God; God is you.

How can you make peace with such a notion? First, by remembering that nothing that enters your mind can be the whole truth.

Reality cannot be conceived.

Words do not apply.

Who You Are

When considering God, truth, or your own identity, questions cannot be answered, statements cannot be accurate.

Nothing can contain that in which all is contained.

At the same time, it may be becoming clearer that who you are, the being that you are, includes *all* things, even the concept of God.

Remember that reality, which is often indicated by the word God, is entirely beyond any images or ideas that could ever exist in the mind. Like you, the reality of God can never be fully apprehended.

When you attempt to use words to express what you know for sure about yourself, you say "I am." In the *Bible*, God's answer to the question of identity is "I am that I am."

See how it works? You are not God; God is you.

Not Two

Who you **are** is nothing you can ever be conscious of, because you are that which contains consciousness.

You are that which makes consciousness possible, not by any effort on your part, but simply because there is only one and you are necessarily that one, because you are, because the being that you are is the one being that manifests as all there is.

All is one. There is only one being and it exists, in its entirety, as who you are.

Feel it right now. Feel what you always are, what you have always been. Do you see how nothing else exists except as it arises in this primordial awareness that is only present because you are? If you were not here, none of this would be happening. It is so simple and so subtle and so literally beyond belief. There is no room for thought here.

Everything is because you are.

Who You Are

Everything is because you are; not the "you" that was born a while ago, that has a name and address, not the "you" whose days are numbered. This is the natural source of all the confusion about who and what you are. You are not temporary. You are that nameless reality in which everything arises, including your body, this universe and this mind through which you are experiencing this moment.

All of your images of who you really are miss the point entirely. All of your cherished concepts about the ultimate truth of life miss the point entirely. The truth is far beyond all images and concepts. *You are the truth*. You are not any kind of entity that can be pointed to or even thought about, yet here you are.

Everything that is, is in you. The awareness that you are in this moment is the presence of being. There *is* no other presence, no other awareness. All states of consciousness, high or low, appear and disappear within this being-awareness that is your ultimate identity.

Not Two

In spite of the resistance you may feel to the incredible notion that you alone exist, the reality of your existence as the source of everything will not go away. You can deny it for as long as you live, but you can never escape the final fact that this being that you are, in this timeless present moment, *is* the one being.

You can verify this right now by acknowledging the simple feeling of being that exists nowhere else but in you. It *is* you. Anything else that appears to exist, anything at all, comes into existence by virtue of the being that you are. You can feel this being right now. Being is one. All beings are this being. You are nothing but this being.
All is one. You are the one.

You are not your thoughts, you are not your feelings, you are not your body. You cannot define yourself in any way, and this moment is a perfect opportunity to stop trying.

You do not exist as an individual being within this universe; this universe exists within the being that you are. The universe exists in you and as you.

Who You Are

In the heart of being, there is perfection beyond any knowing. It is as near as your very self. You are the eye through which the universe sees itself.

You do not need to be on a path.
You have nowhere to go, you are already here.

Here is not a place. Here is what you are.

There is nothing to become, there is nothing you are not. You are absolutely complete in this moment. Why wait for some other moment? Any and all moments can only exist in this timeless moment.

Your past and future exist only in your mind, both illusions, products of memory and imagination.

Reality exists only right now.

Now is not in time. Now is what you are.

PART III

PRACTICE

So what now? How to proceed?

Fortunately, there is no need to decide what to do next. It is not necessary to take up some step-by-step program of self-improvement in order to prepare yourself to live up to the reality of who you are. You lack nothing. You already are who you are.

Once you have recognized the self-effulgent being that is the heart of your existence and once you are able to acknowledge and accept the reality of your inherent being, your job is done. You are carried along by the same current that gives life to the elements and light to those illumined ones who have realized this truth.

Who You Are

From this point on, you will find yourself marveling at the miracle of your life as it is absorbed by degrees into the whole.

As your attention becomes gradually fixed in the reality of your eternal presence, your life in the world proceeds with a subtle grace and harmony that is the natural result of unfettered being.

If you feel the need for help, help will come, often in subtle and unexpected forms.

It is not necessary to search for spiritual teachers to assist you in this practice, especially if you make the choice to *do what they did*. They looked in the only place where ultimate reality can be found, they looked within themselves. They realized their inherent completeness, their unspeakable actuality, beyond all conditions and qualities. They simply turned within and waited patiently for thoughts to settle down, until they found themselves absorbed in that quiescence of mind which is the doorway to the absolute.

Practice

If you should, however, continue to feel the need for a teacher, she or he will appear in your life when you are able and ready to recognize them. Priest or plumber, meditation master or busy mother, you will happen upon one another as a result of the same miracle that puts eggs in the nest and stars in the sky. Then, usually in the language of their own realization, he or she will persistently repeat their interpretation of this same message of love to you until you recognize the simple truth of the innate radiance of the being that you already are.

Any teacher will tell you that it is always beneficial, both for you and for everyone you will ever meet, to make it your daily practice to turn inward toward the ever-present stillness at your center and abide there.

Distilled to its essence, this is the practice; the practice of being.

Who You Are

In this practice it is usually the incessant stream of thoughts that seems to be the biggest obstacle. But your thoughts are just the natural byproduct of the routine operation of the body-mind, just the internal version of the noise of traffic in the street. If you are identified with your mind and body, the thoughts seem real and relevant, but once you understand that they are *only thoughts*, they begin to lose their importance and their potency.

The obstacles that appear in your path *are* your path. Except for them, your job is done, and, believe it or not, in spite of them, your job is already done.

There is nothing you have to do to prepare yourself to be what you are. The happy truth that awakening reveals is that you always already are that which you were so busy wishing and struggling to become. Do you find that you are still wishing and struggling? Then you are ripe in this moment to recognize the *awareness* of the struggle. You are this awareness.

What you are right now…is it.

Practice

The religious temperament is perfectly at home in this practice of being. Worshipping God is focusing the whole of your attention upon the divine presence and experiencing that presence in every aspect of your life and in every moment.

Prayer is being in God's presence. Prayer is listening.
Quieting the mind, opening the heart—opening, opening, naked, undisguised, surrendered without reservation.

Prayer is stillness. No need to think or do or say…anything.

God knows how you feel and what you would say. God knows what is in your heart far better than you do. This is not just because God knows your heart or even because God is in your heart.

The simple truth is that God *is* your heart.

Remember, it is impossible for you to know the whole of anything, while God *is* the whole of everything.

Who You Are

The foundation of this practice is simply being attuned and attentive to your own inherent existence, your presence, your being.

Presence *is* the practice.

Just abide as the being that you are and you *are* that presence.

Remember, God is reality.

God is beyond all definitions, beyond all descriptions, beyond knowing, beyond any imagining.

Even the most ecstatic and overwhelming vision of the unspeakable perfection and limitless glory of God reveals but a feeble glimmer of the infinite truth.

God is infinite truth, and truth, far beyond our capacity to know it, is God.

Practice

The practice of being could not be simpler: be what you are. How hard can that be? Well, in theory, since you already are what you are, it's "mission accomplished." But your true identity as nameless and unchanging reality is completely unaffected by your ideas about this ultimate truth. The fact that you embody and manifest the nexus of infinite being and nonbeing is, by now, old news. There is nothing extraordinary here. Every person, every puppy, every pebble, every proton is part of and *all* of the great miracle of being here.

So what are you going to do about it? Perhaps a better question would be, Is it necessary to do anything about it? Ultimately, no. But considering it relatively, as a member of the human family, wouldn't it be nice to appreciate what is happening and be free and clear enough to be able to help one another? In fact, as you continue to harmonize with life through the conscious practice of being, you will find yourself naturally living for the welfare of all. Why? Because each *is* all.

You are everyone.

Who You Are

This practice is simply abiding as the being that you always are. One way to go about being what you are is to carry on as you always have, business as usual. If it is true that you already *are* everything you could ever become, why not just rest in that and let nature take its course. Reality is no less real, truth no less true.

But what about you? Has your recent "business as usual" carried with it the sense of happiness and peace that is reported to accompany the state of being in harmony with one's self? Does love abound in your life? How do you feel? Are you whole, are you integrated, are you all of a piece? If you are, then you have already found your way to some substantial measure of this presence, whether it be through your relationship to yourself and the universe or through a genuine relationship with God that has eclipsed the call for self-inquiry.

But if there seem to be some pieces missing, this practice will point you in a helpful direction and give a whole new meaning to the phrase, "let nature take its course."

Practice

Turning your attention back in its own direction takes a significant amount of will and concentration, especially after the first few attempts. Initially you are fueled by the energy of the experiment and the promise of the great awakenings and moments of bliss that are said to be a part of looking within, of realizing yourself. Later, after you have learned to rest in the stillness from which your experience arises, the simultaneous calming and energizing effects of this presence will provide the enthusiasm necessary to continue.

This practice can be undertaken anywhere, anytime. Just withdraw your attention from the external events that are happening around you and focus your attention on the silent center. If you are able, you can keep your attention on outer events of your day *and* simultaneously remain aware of the primordial being that is the ground and source of everything that is happening. But in the early going, it is very difficult to look deeply into your ever-present presence unless you have abandoned all your other activities for the moment. And that sounds a lot like meditation.

Who You Are

Meditation is another word that carries many meanings. The dictionary will tell you that meditation is deep, continuous thought, reflection, and contemplation. Yet most people who practice some form of meditation will tell you that they are not so interested in entertaining deep thoughts as they are in becoming free of thoughts altogether. This has to be one of the most difficult challenges anyone can undertake. If you think not, try it for thirty seconds.

The benefits to be gained from the physical, mental, emotional, and spiritual effects of meditation are difficult to overestimate. There already exists an abundance of scientific and anecdotal evidence to support the unparalleled value of meditation in every avenue of life, and yet only a tiny percentage of people choose to take advantage of this consummate practice and to enjoy these inestimable benefits.

Do you wonder why?

Practice

If you currently have a daily meditation practice or if you have tried meditation in the past, you already know why people don't meditate. Especially in the early weeks of practice, most people find it *very* difficult. There are many people who abandon the attempt to practice meditation after the first two or three sessions. It's that tough! Spending 3 hours in a grueling workout at the gym is a stroll in the park compared to twenty minutes of sitting completely still without some entertainment.

Some of the most common forms of meditation focus the attention on sounds, words, phrases, questions, prayers, or the use of prayer beads, all techniques employed to restrain the normally undisciplined mind. Other popular methods recommend closely following the breath as it goes in and out of the nose or attending to the rising and falling of the abdomen, while others encourage counting the breaths as an aid to developing the ability to fix the mind on a single point. Some more advanced meditation techniques employ complex visualizations or the perception and manipulation of subtle energies, while other advanced methods are causal in nature and are generally understood to be formless.

Who You Are

A few of the many varieties of meditation are intended to stimulate and cultivate specific states of consciousness and the experiences that accompany them. Most methods, however, emphasize the development of one-pointed concentration which will naturally result in a progressive quieting of the body and the mind.

The majority of people who practice meditation employ one of the concentrative methods. In this approach to meditation you are instructed to concentrate on a designated focus of attention to the exclusion of all else. Anytime your attention wanders from the assigned object of concentration, a sound or your breath, for example, you are guided to acknowledge the appearance of the mental image and to return immediately to the task at hand without creating any additional mental activity through analysis or judgment of the content of the mental moment. You are also cautioned to avoid indulging in judgments and self-criticism which can arise because your mind has wandered yet again.

Practice

This procedure will eventually result in a relatively quiet mind. As the mind becomes less and less active, there will be occasional periods of complete stillness. These periods of stillness often go unnoticed because the mind has fallen silent, so there is no "mind" present to notice them. Sometimes, however, when the mind emerges from these moments of silence, thoughts or sensations may reappear in the form of insights or subtle positive feelings. These are clear indicators of your nearness to that silent center, that empty fullness from which everything arises.

When you find yourself in this position, and you will, this is not the time to return to a focus of concentration. The reason you are this close to stillness is because the mind has finally settled down enough to allow you to feel the presence of the great ocean of being that you always are. Now there is no need to *do* anything.

Just be where you are.
Just be what this is.
Just be.
This is the practice.

Who You Are

The meditative approach is entirely appropriate to the practice of apprehending the core of your being. It is probably the best way to undertake this practice because, especially in the beginning, it takes a strong focus of concentration to keep your eye trained on itself. It requires holding very still and paying close attention, and the best way to do this is to stay in one place for a while and cultivate a meditative mindset.

True meditation is utter stillness; abiding as the silent witness of the ever-changing mind and the ever-changing world.

Here is a simple method for beginning meditation: First, find a relatively quiet place where you are least likely to be interrupted and then choose a comfortable position so that your body will not intrude.

Most meditators find it helpful if the spine is straight, but don't worry about your posture for the moment. It is likely that your body will reorganize itself quite naturally as you continue.

Practice

Take a few moments to become aware of your body and senses in order to fix yourself squarely in the present moment. Once you feel situated, recall that this practice is focused on the mind and especially on that which lies beyond the mind.

Now the practice, and the fun, can begin. You know the drill: Take your attention off the world "out there," including even your own body, and turn it back upon itself. No specific object of concentration at all except the vastness of your infinite, unborn, and indescribable being.

Just stop what you are doing and don't start anything else. Simply watch yourself exist.

If your intention is to discover reality, look no further. Just keep your attention trained on what you are. No need to ask Who am I? The question dissolves in your own direct experience of the unfathomable presence that you are. If you were to ask, "What is this?" The answer: "*This* is what this is." No descriptions, no explanations. This is this. This is it.

Who You Are

As you continue in this practice, your mind will wander, given that you're human. But these thoughts do not have to be a problem. They are as natural as the ever-moving air, sometimes calm and sometimes blustery, with the occasional tornado thrown in just to keep you humble. Yet the reality that you are is never apart from you, it *is* you, so there is no need to struggle to stay on task.

Just keep gently returning to what you always are.

There are times, however, when "gently returning" will seem nearly impossible. There is nothing that appears in nature that is any wilder or more unruly than the human mind, so you need not be surprised or frustrated when it seems difficult to find your way to where you really are. Your mind will repeatedly try to lure you into a trip down memory lane or into some future-oriented fantasy land. Simply decline the invitation.

If you want to avoid getting stuck in a conceptual quagmire, you are probably going to need some sort of homing device to lead you back into the present moment.

Practice

The contemplative traditions offer a variety of techniques to help you regain your center. Among these are visualization and mantra, both powerful remedies for the wandering mind but both requiring some special training to be used most effectively. Another alternative is the breath. From the Latin *spiritus,* the breath can only happen in this moment and is an ideal homing device. Remember, though, that the breath is not the focus of your meditation, you are. Once you have regained your center, the breathing will take care of itself

The most direct method for finding your way through the mental noise is to come back to the one thing you know for sure: you are. Whatever the thoughts, feelings, or sense impressions that assert themselves into your consciousness, they appear *because you are*. Hold onto that beingness. Your bare existence is the beacon that lights your way, the anchor that keeps you from drifting off when the winds of the world are blowing.

Beyond all your ideas of who you are, you come upon the experience of utter this-ness.

Who You Are

What you are doing here is bringing into awareness the fact that you are. First you acknowledge this awareness of being and ultimately pass beyond awareness into the fact itself.

When you enter into the fact of being, this practice comes to fruition. You are no longer looking within. There is no difference between inside and outside. Your boundaries have disappeared into the fact of being. Then you no longer even know that you are, you just are. You don't become anything new, you simply stop imagining.

Illusions vanish in the clear light of what is.

It should not require a lot of discipline to do this, but the fruits of this practice are less likely to grow and ripen without a conscious decision to adopt and maintain a regular practice. If you find this practice arduous or tedious, you may want to take a break. Chances are good that you will take it up again.

Practice

Those who feel they must control themselves with discipline and deprivation in order to follow a "spiritual path" are missing the point. You do not take up the practice of being because you think you should be on a spiritual path.

There is no path to where you already are.

Finding yourself in this natural kinship with reality, you begin to lose interest in the make-and-believe world that had been so seductive and so hypnotic.

While it may appear that discipline is called for in the early stages of this practice, you eventually discover that the need for self-control is superseded by an irresistible fascination that gradually evolves into earnestness and devotion.

There is also more than a little intrigue involved, because no matter how much you discover, you sense that there will always be infinitely more to be discovered, and you notice that, as you experience the fruits of the practice appearing in your life, everything just keeps getting better.

Who You Are

Once you have become present in your body and centered in your mind, you can turn your attention inward and gaze into the incomprehensible vastness that you are. Just see what is. Feel what is happening. Watch as consciousness becomes conscious of itself. See that vastness revealed, the infinity that only nothing can contain.

First you behold the fullness and emptiness, then you recognize what this is. You realize that this is not just another experience, one among many; this is the source from which everything arises and into which everything returns. This is not some *thing* you are seeing; you are the seer, the seeing, and the seen. This is you, this wordless, unborn, boundless presence into which "you" are absorbed so completely that there is only this, only what is.

And from this pristine actuality a steady stream of love and inexpressible joy flows forth, born of your very existence.

The bliss of being.

Practice

The life that you were living when you began this practice will now be lived by your body, mind, and heart as "you" dissolve into what always is.

You were not born into this life to live eternally; you are beyond time altogether. There was no beginning, there can be no end. You are not someone who lives and dies. You are not merely a person; you are in every moment the transpersonal and entirely transcendent reality that manifests as being.

This is not a difficult practice. Once you have been at it for a while you may notice that while nothing in your outer world has changed very much, everything seems different somehow and better.

And all it takes is a few minutes devoted to the direct experience of your inherent being. Just remember that there is nothing to search for, nothing incomplete, nothing left undone, and then rest in what always already is.

Who You Are

Once you have learned to recognize this simple fact of being, it will be easier to differentiate it from the myriad objects that appear within it.

Just a few seconds of stillness will make a difference; a minute or two will make a big difference. Like panning for gold, a stream of thoughts may flow by before you find your way to this shining stillness, only to be immediately swept away again by another thought or daydream. Not to worry.

Remember, stillness is not your goal; stillness is merely a point of access to the inaccessible. Why inaccessible? Because you cannot "get to" where you already are.

Whether your mind is busy or still, you already are what you have always been. It is impossible to "become" what you already are.

Like the lost eyeglasses that are already on your face, the trick is to find what you have not lost.
That's why it's called realization.

Practice

There are sincere participants in various religions who believe that cultivating an empty space within opens the door for darkness to creep in and ultimately overcome the unwary soul who opens that forbidden gate.

Anyone who has been involved with meditation or silent prayer for a while will tell you that those beliefs are not far from the truth.

If you already have some experience with spiritual practices, you may have discovered that it usually takes only a few hours of practice, and sometimes only a few minutes, before the shadows begin to emerge from the deep places within where they have been hunkered down, many of them sequestered there since childhood. This is not fun. Some of the memories and realizations that may arise in your awareness can be *very* unpleasant and even painful. That is why they ended up as shadows in the first place. Sometimes when bad things happened, you could not feel that much pain all at once, so some of it was postponed, repressed, or denied altogether.

Who You Are

A stable inner silence can appear only after all the noise has gone away. This means that both the hounds of hell *and* the heralds of heaven must fall silent. It may seem easier to let the painful shadows go, but it is just as necessary to also release the blissful feelings if you would make room for the true quiet.

Stillness is the doorway to reality. Reality includes everything. The darkness inside must come to the surface and the light within will also come to the surface. Each arises from and dissolves into stillness, a stillness which may seem from a distance to be utter nothingness; but it is from such perfect darkness that reality dawns.

When reality is seen as two, the opposites come into being: subject and object, positive and negative, inner and outer, darkness and light; they all spring to life together. Reality includes all of it. Not just the relative truths of objective existence, but also the absolute truth that is timelessly transcendent and nondual.

Not two, not even one. Beyond beyond.

Practice

If you try to think about this, you only create a new thought, and that thought, however exalted, can only lead you away from the ineffable truth.

Reality already is. Let it be.

Ultimately, there is no practice to this practice. You have already understood that what you are cannot be known, and that you already are what that is. The practice is not knowing anything. The practice is being everything.

The practice is being.

And here you find yourself; nothing to think, no adequate words, and often with emotions so immense that they make you feel as if you had been stunned. All in all, a very good place from which to continue. Continue what? Well, continue with your life. Go back to work, have something to eat, take a walk, call a friend, or maybe get some sleep. When you awaken, you may find that you are just a little more awake.

FRUITS OF PRACTICE

As you continue in this practice of revisiting the central fact of your being, wonderful insights will arise spontaneously and little miracles will play themselves out as a natural result of your growing attunement to reality.

If you undertake this one thing in earnest, all other aspects of your life will evolve of their own accord. Serendipitous events will become commonplace and your life and relationships will unfold with a grace and harmony that arise from a source beyond knowing.

You may notice that the things you find yourself saying and doing are more loving and more helpful than anything you could have orchestrated by your own design. A natural symmetry will begin to appear in your life in which circumstances and events seem to be tailored to your specific needs or intentions.

Who You Are

You will also find yourself in situations that bring your liabilities into focus. You may suddenly understand how you have been getting in your own way and you will realize that life is presenting you with opportunities to choose new ways of relating to challenging circumstances.

If you are a person who is often irritable, experiencing waves of frustration or anger; you may discover a more even temperament emerging. If you have been impatient or aggressive, you may find a new composure seeping into your thoughts and your behavior.

If you are usually shy and passive, an unfamiliar sense of purpose and determination may begin to take command in your life. If you are nervous or restless, peace will appear of its own accord. If your energy is low and you still maintain this practice, a welcome enthusiasm will become apparent. Poor health habits will begin to correct themselves naturally, as unwise choices fall away and the body's energy increases.

The Fruits of Practice

Unhappiness, doubt, distrust, and fear, all gradually replaced by love; love that insinuates itself into your life without any conscious effort on your part, except as you continue each day to rest in the light of your own immaculate and quite ordinary presence.

Your emotions will follow a similar course. Initially you may experience a heightened sensitivity, feeling emotions more deeply and being affected by things that used to pass unnoticed. Then you discover that the many feelings that were the palate of your emotional life are gradually being replaced by boundless love that overwhelms the power of all other emotions like the sun shining on candlelight.

This doesn't imply that you will cease to feel; rather, it heralds the opening of your heart to the all-embracing and altogether unspeakable love that is your true heart.

Who You Are

As you continue to bask in the light of being you will blossom as naturally as any flower and you will feel the effects in every part of your life.

When in the company of other people, you may begin to notice an increasing sense of intimacy, empathy, and compassion. You may eventually hear another person say that you seem to know what is in their heart and you will understand that it is not their heart you know, but your own. For in reality, there is only one heart, one mind, one spirit, one being.

The central practice that makes all the difference is the simple return to the heart of being that is always and everywhere, who you are.

The Fruits of Practice

So take your attention, which is usually busy with objects of perception, and train that attention instead upon the subject, upon the perceiver of those objects.

It is important to understand that the objects that are being perceived include *all* objects, and this means you. It means that anything you perceive as being yourself cannot be yourself because in the instant of perception, it becomes an object. Remember, you are the subject and, as such, can never be seen.

As you continue in the practice of observing yourself, you are constantly discarding every object that appears. Eventually, objects cease arising and only the subject remains. But the subject, without an object to give it existence, also disappears, and only the one, the non-dual, remains.

When the duality of subject and object dissolves, all things are profoundly not two, and you are nowhere to be found.

Who You Are

When you have dissolved into this reality, even the one ceases to exist. There is only what is, beyond all definitions, beyond any sense of identity.

There is no one to say "I am," there is only what is, the absolute, beyond all forms and qualities; timeless, nameless, conditionless, perfect, ultimate reality. And this absolute reality is manifest in whatever is before you in each moment of your life.

Naturally, in the midst of this stateless state, questions or confusion about God and self, being and non-being, do not arise. If you continue in this practice of consciously living in your own unqualified presence, you will find you have less and less interest in all such questions; not because you have given up trying to answer them, but because the questions have ceased to be questions and you are no longer trying to explain how things are.

After all, what can you say about that which is beyond words?

The Fruits of Practice

Absolute reality exists not just in you, but as you, as the being that you are. As you continue to live ever more deeply in awareness of changeless and ever-present being, the questions and quandaries that plague humankind will cease to have meaning for you, except as love compels you to live in a way that helps relieve the suffering of a dreaming world.

AFTERWORD

Who you are
is the secret of life.

The secret of life is hidden
only by proximity.

It is an open secret.
It is right in front of your face.
It is right behind your eyes.
It is everywhere.
Precious beyond any price
and free for all.

The secret of life
is you.

Be still and know…

ACKNOWLEDGMENTS

Profound and unending gratitude to the many men and women, past and present, who have communicated to us this most precious confidence, the inmost desire of every heart.

Many thanks to Ian Kloss, Christina Laurel, Edmund and Florence Kloss, John VanLare, Corey Vance, Toinette Lippe, Cedric Grigg, and Robert Carwithen. These are the people who provided the guidance that brought this book to life.

INDEX

Index

Index

Index

Index

priest, 89
proposition, 69-70
proton, 93
proximity, 123
psychology, 68
pulse, 51
puppy, 93
questions, 118, 119
reality, 5, 13-4, 73, 75, 79, 82, 84, 92, 110-1,
      118-9
Realization, 108
religion, 67-8, 74, 109
restless, 114
science, 15, 55, 67-70
sciens, 69
secret of life, 123
seeing, 38-9, 43, 64
self-improvement, 87
self-realization, 51, 61, 73
separateness, 78
shadows, 109
shy, 114
silence, 63, 110
silly question, 8
sophia, 67
soul, 26
space, 44, 55
spine, 100
spirit, 116
spiritual, 67, 68
spiritual path, 105
spiritual teacher, 88-9
spiritus, 103

Index

LaVergne, TN USA
25 October 2009
161946LV00003BA/180/P